Stars Glimmer

Stars Glimmer

poems by
Judith Heilizer

CALUMET EDITIONS

Minneapolis

First Edition November 2023
Stars Glimmer
Copyright 2023 Judith Heilizer
All rights reserved.

10 9 8 7 6 5 4 3 2 1

ISBN 978-1-962834-02-5

Cover design: Gary Lindberg

Also by this Author

The Sun Rises as Does the Moon

Contents

The Letters of the Alphabet   1
Apothecary   2
I Am So Afraid   8
Birthday   9
Clutter   11
Colors   13
Coming Home   14
Emergency Room   16
Floating   18
Garbo   19
Guppy   20
I Changed You   22
It Was Not Really Fair   23
Lending Library   24
Life (a Conversation with God)   25
Love   27
Loving   28

Memorial Day Paradox   29
Mirror   32
Mobius (two-person conversation)   34
More and Less   36
Newspaper   38
Opposites   39
Random Thoughts   40
See Saw   41
Silence   42
Some Day   43
Thanks Taking   45
Time   46
Tiny Murders   48
Toolkit   50
Trusting   52
Viewing Point   53
War and Peace   55
Why   57

The Letters of the Alphabet

The letters of the alphabet
are like a large family

together by design
not by choice
about whom comes before the other
and who follows

some are silent, others make sounds
when they hold hands they make words
whose task it is to inform us
or to join us together
or to divide us
depending on what is needed
the letters of the alphabet have helpers
whose job it is to bring order and meaning to the words
dots and commas
and question marks and explanation points

my favorite group is:
RUOK?
Four letters holding us in their care.

Apothecary

He was the usual cut and dry apothecary, of no particular age and color with a strong Edinburgh accent and about as emotional as a bagpipe.

from *The Strange Case of Dr. Jekyll and Mr. Hyde,* Robert Louis Stevenson

He is the bland man in the white coat behind the grey counter
in front of the grey
wall with the white cubicles labelled A–Z in
black letters
against the grey back wall of the what-not store

He has neatly trimmed hair, usually sandy-grey
wears unoffending glasses, nails
neatly trimmed straight across
has a light band of skin around
his ring finger where
the wedding band lives when he is not at work
wears a white polyester jacket with his name and credential embroidered in
grey on the left chest pocket

He glides to and fro behind the grey mottled
counter, eyes fixed alternately on bits of white
paper or on the grey computer screen

When you on the other side of the grey counter have need of his
    attention
you generally have to clear your throat
politely
sometimes more than once, which
will eventually cause him to stick out his hand for
your little bit of paper,
and cause his eyes to dart back and forth between
it and the computer
never at you

When he mumbles: Wait? You slide away
wander about the store, buy stuff you don't need, might even
hate
come back to the other end of the grey mottled counter when
you hear your name (you usually miss the first call).

Once there someone hands you an envelope with
a container and miles of printed matter which you eagerly reach for,
    but
the bland man comes sliding between you and it and
asks: do you have any questions, then usually
glides away before you have had enough time to remember any
He has not looked at you

My father, who looked like a father, was a druggist so to speak.
He conceded to the white linen jacket without writing on the
    pocket, nothing else was
asked for.

He sold things for the body and things for the soul, good
smelling and good feeling
things and occasionally something from an
unlabeled drawer

What I remember most are the scents
the wall behind the counter filled with brass bins of herbs, sweet and
    savory and
bitter and sour, and
crispy and crumbly and greyish and greenish

My father has a little shovel with which he
measures out the flora singly
or in combinations in little
brown paper bags
meets out healing for whatever you need

He is friend and confidant and preacher

What my father is not is a trained pharmacist.
My mother is

So when a doctor's prescription needs to be filled, he
pushes a button discretely lodged under the counter, which
causes my mother to emerge from our apartment behind
the store, she
throws on a white jacket which
hangs in the hall

embroidered with her credentials
fills said prescription, then melts
back into the kitchen as
my father rings it up

It all works

My father-in-law was a pharmacist. He too
dealt in all manner of prescriptives, I am told
But he had two additional virtues. In the front of the store
there was an honest to goodness soda fountain which
dispensed fizzies and other sweet concoctions while you
waited. It was a sort of gathering place, where coincidentally
you brought your medicinal needs

But you got way more than that. You got
friendship. You got community. You got care for the body as well as
    for the soul

When he wasn't busy my father-in-law studied the Jewish sages or
    the Quakers.

In addition he dispensed a favorite
concoction he had designed. Named Russlax
It was an admixture of the wine he was granted
for his apothecary during prohibition
and some Russian herbs, which his family bottled in
brown lightproof bottles, which

he labeled, wrapped in cellophane and dispensed as a foolproof
laxative

But wait, this was a full-service establishment. His wife
cooked soups and made sandwiches which
she sold at a loss to the laborers

I want to know
Who are these people, these guardians of our wellbeing?

These all are keepers of our secrets, know more about
you than
perhaps they should, might unravel your
genetics, could
piece together where
and with whom you might have been and whether
you should have. Know your emotional demons or whether
you are pregnant or impotent or dying, might be able to
judge how much time you might have left, can
slow down or speed up the flow of
help, may even save our life, may
have your past and present and future in their hands

So I wonder
would I rather be cared for by Mr. Computer and
his right hand, the Bland Man?
or would I rather be held by

more warmly colored care
and less
tech?

I know the answer, but
I would rather not say it out loud.

I Am So Afraid

of not being able to remember
the luminescence of the dragonfly's wings in the sunlight

of only being able to remember
how blind I was when the light faded

of not being able to remember
the pirouetting glimmers dancing into the water

of only being able to remember darkness
because it is easier to remember than light

of not being able to remember that love becomes invisible
if we barter it to those few we deem deserving

of only being able to remember what we have received
shrinking our gifts to measure for measure

of remembering
and of not remembering

Spirit

please send us memory

the dragonfly's wings shimmer in the sunlight.

Birthday

I awake into my birthday
      Please nobody notice
            I have much to do about that

For starters
I would like to know who my mother was then
Was she lying on her bed, moaning in anguish, or, perhaps in pleasure, as she pushed me
away from her?

Had she moaned in anguish or in pleasure those nine months sooner?
Had she pushed him away also, but perhaps too soon or not soon enough?

After empty space
A clothesline of memories, wrinkled or fuzzy or smooth with sharp edges
Flapping in the breeze
A basketful more, some folded, others bunched or drawn thin
Still waiting to be hung

Passing by the shriveling face in the mirror, overindulgent rage
At shrinking looks and time and chances
The raucous emptiness of things unsaid, undone
Then
Dawning into the here and now
The simpleness of gratitude, placebo for personal bankruptcy

The children are so forgiving, it aches Do you not see how I failed you?
Please blame me
I do

Then after the blaming, send me your clemency

If not mercy

I can't.

Clutter

Have you noticed
our secret love affair
with mess and clutter

mind you, this is not dirt love,
that is awful, unattractive, nasty
this is just about stuff
that happens to be in our world,
the gloves, separated, on the sofa
the hat tossed onto the coffee table
perhaps an unacknowledged secret delight
of memories of childhood, getting away with naughtiness
these stealthy visitors who make themselves at home
in our spaces
unknown, unseen
until we wake to the
awareness of the too much clutter

and so we judge and toss and save
until there seems to be some order
for a little while
until the other takes over again

so it is also in our inner world
the mess and clutter of living with ourselves,
of self judgement called on for help
the endless refrain of demands, leaving little space
for holding ourselves

simply
for self-love

so let us toss and save
until we are truly who we are
leaving us free
to be
just that.

Colors

Have you noticed
there are no clashing colors in nature
adjacent hues complement each other
bring out the best
which had remained hidden until they were paired.

So it can be with our relationships
which can bring out the best in one another
when they are paired

But too often
we tend to force things together
ignoring
that they were intended to remain separated
and then everyone loses

So let us learn the gentle lesson of Nature:
There is no place
for clashing colors

Coming Home

A droplet of water
separating itself
from its host
the water in the Universe
eternally unchanging

curious the droplet is
nosy if you will
so it floats to where it is being taken
unwilling to resist

you need a lesson
says the water
go, be on your own
and so it does

unexpectedly
the droplet's surroundings change
grow colder
the droplet changes with it
becomes chrystalline
like others of its kind
turns into a snowflake
is drawn to the ground
and is called
snow

until the sun pours out her warmth
and the flakes become water once more

so it is with our ventures
let us not loose contact with who we were
before we ventured out

change can be good
but let us be careful not to disconnect
from the source
from who we were meant to be
forever

Emergency Room

An unplanned misstep at the top of the staircase

the unintended descent down the steps
the requisite bruises swelling over the injury site

a fast trip to the comforting emergency room
close by

the space contains a well matched set
of needers and givers
those folk trained in setting things right
at least for this moment in this space

the check in accomplished in low voices
designed to protect the nakedness of the patient

the occupants eye each arrival,
create some story
and draw back into their own space

parents shush their children, grownups stroke their loved ones
the atmosphere designed to be what it is not
an ordinary place where one just happens to be

the little girl runs around the room, making her barf bag flutter
some people look around the space trying to get and give
    reassurance
others move deeply inside a space only they can enter
all waiting to be called into the magical healing room

the older man lies on the floor, thrashing, yelling, intoxicated
the young man moves restlessly around in his chair
apparently having overdosed
his shorts, socks and shoes are in the policewoman's possession
her gun freely accessible to her, just in case,
while they chat like friends
in this unlikely meeting place…

this is where we go
when our edges become too frayed
and all we need is the promise
that we will be held and healed.

Floating

The drop of water separates
from all the water of the world
up there, where it was born

it makes the long journey earthward
slower at times, more rapidly at others
gently or bumpily
depending on conditions and needs
and sometimes just on desires
where it becomes of the stuff of the Universe
once more

so it is with us

born of the water
we float through our lives
at varying speeds
creating contents by choice
or by circumstance

still,
we return to the earth
the outcome predictable
for each living thing.

Garbo

Staring into the looking glass of her mind with empty eyes, finding
only photographs on billboards, processed smiles or frowns or
    blankness
dead in a way, gorgeously dead,
really wishing, maybe

to find some flaw, or a muscle twitch, or the slightest promise of
    some life
but all the faces are fixed forever in their cage of youth and practiced
    emotions
copied
and scientifically emulated and airbrushed to approach the real thing
as closely as possible

The space around her carefully emptied of anything that breathes or
    moves or
might want to attach, heaven forbid

I am private, I live like a monk with a toothbrush and a pot of
    cream, private joys and sorrows will cheapen when you share
    them, don't succumb, don't even look at your own works,
    remain separate

I want to be alone. No, wait, I meant I want to be left alone,
honestly, that is what I meant

But that was then and this is now…
Will celluloid bend itself around my body and keep me warm like
    an embrace or warm feathers?

Oh no, don't go there, hold on a little longer, you will make it.

Guppy

The last day of school
eagerly anticipated
by teachers and children alike
more so
as the air conditioning had failed
perhaps less so by parents

the school fair
putting a period
between the year that was
and the much better one to be, hopefully
games and food
and the inevitable summer take home
of class pets and plants
and all things perishable

my little son volunteers us
to take the guppy captured on a field trip
miraculously still alive
after a week in a glass jar
on the class windowsill

the guppy comes with instructions for wellness care and guppy food
but without a name

my son instantly names it
Jaws

my little son loves the guppy
reluctantly agrees
to a family weekend away
makes sure the guppy will be well supplied

when we return the guppy floats lifeless
on the bottom of the jar

I had so hoped I could protect him
from learning the unlearnable lesson
of endings

I had failed

we find a sunny spot at the base of a tree
where the guppy will do its work
of nourishing the dandelions
you love to pick
through his tears
my little son smiles.

I Changed You

I changed you
into what I needed you to be
you did not protest
it was all so easy

but then you began to notice the imbalance
between your giving and my taking
and you demanded
equality

I could not be there in that way for you

It was not that I could not see the logic
I just had nothing to give you

and so you left

now it is how it was
before you were part of me

except that you left a gaping hole in me
instead of you

I miss you so.

It Was Not Really Fair

I trotted out all my goodies… brainish, devilish, sexy

He had no clue about what I was doing
that I was just in it for the fun of it, nothing more

So I caught him as I knew I would
Practice makes perfect

Charming he was and interested and eager
It was so easy, too easy in fact
But the pleasure of its working made it still worthwhile

Will you go to dinner and to the symphony with me?
They are playing Beethoven
Please leave me a message, here is my number…

…Sure, I am thinking, another notch on my unavailability gun…

I dial…
"Fuer Elise" sings the machine, "please leave me a message …."

I have lost
l am his

It wasn't really fair.…

Lending Library

Life is a lending library
We work our way through the stacks
Free to choose any title
That reflects our self-view
Or challenges us
I am
I am not
I want to be
I don't want to be
or anything in between

There is no fee
All Life asks of us
Is not to lose our library card.

Life (a Conversation with God)

If You give me something
we call it Life
and I know for sure
You will ask me
to give it back

Is it a loan
or a gift?

If it is a loan
I know that
I will have to return it
because You keep records
of what is owed You
and You insist on repayment
that is only fair

You put out forewarnings,
a lesser body, greying hair
(which I can choose to ignore)
so You rev up the information
until I receive it

But I can imagine
that You might forget about a gift
for a while
(and I hope forever)
and that I get to use it
(until You remember to check your gift ledger…)

What is clear is that You are in charge

After the struggle
My self-congratulatory flirtation
with acceptance

Then the noise dies down
until the next time

Just being with what is…

Love

There is this time
when the boundary
between the other and our self

becomes softly blurred
and we call it intimacy

it is a place mostly empty of words
though there may be sounds
and likely also touching
and we call it desire

it is a time and a place
in which we might loose ourselves
in the being of the other
and we call it home

we have known of this place forever
though we may never have been there before
and we call it

love.

Loving

Have you noticed
how differently we feel
when we are in love
from when we love someone?

Being in love conveys the possibility
of impermanence
We can fall out of love
Loving someone takes up
all the space inside
There is no room
for anything else.

Memorial Day Paradox

A strange concept this
honoring by remembering the pain of their loss

theirs, the dead, for having lost themselves for us

how does this work?
you can't be in two places at once, there and here
dead but alive to receiving our memorials at the same time

except of course those who have lost parts of themselves only
like arms and legs and the future they had dreamed of before
they get something, I am just not quite sure what that is

it is really we who get something for remembering
sort of doing it for them, paying respects
but mostly making us feel good about ourselves
for our sensitivity to their loss even if they are not able to know of it

Army and Airforce and Marines and Police and Firefighters and
    Dignitaries and Schools and all
manner of folks who make our lives better
marching in the shoes of the silent dead or of the diminished not
    dead

behind me twelve chairs labeled RESERVED FOR HAPPY
    HAVEN NURSING HOME RESIDENTS,
filled with inward looking souls, watching the parade,
seeking to connect to this now and that then, maybe catching it,
    maybe not

Judith Heilizer | *Stars Glimmer*

we clap for these gone ones and whistle
and feel virtuous and compassionate
and perhaps we even make silent bargains with ourselves to
do good deeds
and prevent war
eradicating the need for these folks' sacrifices altogether
this matters

just when our introspection grows heavy and we need relief
there they come
unicyclists and the gymnasts and the kids on decorated bicycles
and a festooned dog here and there
even a rabbit with red, white and blue ears, drawing odd feeling
    laughter

all deemed worthy of walking in those hallowed steps

and the little kids, jumping up from their curb seats
scrambling for the candy showers and the frisbees and the coupons
    for free this's and thats
learning that speed matters to acquisition

and two and a half hours later the very last float
bearing my granddaughter and her friends
students at Miss Maggies Dance Studio,
through it the sounds and noises of all kinds of music
moistening our uncertain senses

and within me then a shout and a prayer

God Bless America
for being just this, just right,
may we keep our innocence

Gratitude

Mirror

Plowed furrows across the woman's forehead
pleated veils draping the outer corners of her eyes
rows of lines fanning out above the nose which looks more pointed
than the nose remembered
dry gullies carved beside the mouth by spent laughter,
cheekbones jutting out above scooped cheeks,
covered with feathered skin of nondescript color
thinning lips, their shape changed from yes to maybe

under her gaze the eyes become a stage on which
curtains slowly part, revealing life lived for better or
for worse, wonderings and imaginings whirling
around with knowings and believings and absent
answers

sometimes her thoughts rummage around
in the whatnot box of her memories,
children mounted like butterflies on
faded photos and wiggling on rickety video tapes,
the forever two-year-old at his own graduation from medical school
the little princess pushing her infant in a stroller

deeper down her self, the bride enfolded in pure white,
not knowing yet that this virginal canvas
will become a palette for the brushes of life or with life
however it will go

before taking leave the woman will ask the eyes
to look into the future
tell me who I will become, who I will cease to be

that is when the curtains slowly close…

we cannot tell the future they say, we are the recorders
you are the architect
we suggest that you go looking elsewhere,
maybe in your heart or in
your soul or in any of the places where you live

but
be sure to bring forgiveness with you

she closes her eyes
and tries to find her way there

and sometimes she comes
just near enough to

almost touch.

Mobius
(two-person conversation)

Do you love me?

        I do

Do you really love me?

        I do really love you

I don't feel loved

        Why?

If you really loved me you would know why I don't feel loved

        But I do love you

How will I know that you love me if you don't know why I don't feel loved

        I need you to tell me what I should do so you will know that I love you

Oh, now it's all about your needs

Now I understand: because I don't know what I need to do so you will know that I love you, you want me to agree that I don't love you because if I do love you I would know what I don't know. Therefore I don't love you

Told you.

More and Less

Sometimes
we look upward
to the treasured Other

they know us in a way we don't
and to which knowing
we can only aspire
some day

for now they have all the answers
know how to soothe and smoothe
our sometimes raggedy inner world
in which they stand
tall and firm

and so we give them all our trust
hold nothing back

until inevitably they fail us, being human
move to a different place in our selves
altogether

we cannot find them
we are alone
again

then the other becomes less
shrinks grotesquely

and so do we
until we find ourselves again
and become more
once more.

Newspaper

Our mind
reads our lives
like we read the newspaper

so much to learn
about what is and was and
is still to be
the news of the day
satisfying or not
depending on expectation and achievement

sometimes
when we are very still
the pages come fluttering by
with or without our desire
or permission

did I measure up to the intention
heralded in yesterday's edition?

each day another paper with more news
each day another record of yesterday
hoping our subscription
will last forever

knowing
that it won't.

Opposites

There is this sense of gratitude
that rests on the contemplation
of its opposite
we come in from the winter's cold
and are grateful for the warmth
we come in from the summer's heat
and are grateful for the coolness
the thermometer reading has not changed
it shows a steady 70 degrees
we search for a snack in the refrigerator
we find yesterday's cold and stiff spaghetti
which has no appeal
we are grateful that our weight loss program
has not been derailed

there is this and then there is it's opposite
and they are both true.

Random Thoughts

Paradox

I pride myself
on being a realist
and so I know that one day
I will cease to be
I want to know this state
make friends with the inevitable
so I try to imagine myself as not existing
but there is a problem:
how can I be the observer of my absent presence
without existing?
how can I make peace with that
without being?
how can I have essence
without leaving a shadow?

See Saw

You and I
are riding on the see-saw
when I push off so I can fly
you drop to the still ground below
you keep me suspended in midair
helpless
unsaid words
thundering between us

when you relent and you let me down
I get to keep you up forever
unless you jump

let us build a see-saw of words
that folds in the middle
so we can be in the same place

together.

Silence

Sometimes
our life with the other
becomes cloudy
the road between us
rutted

we need to be heard
so we can be known

but the other has failed to hear us
talks over us

and so we find ourselves
nonexistent
the inner silence
thick
with emptiness

our words lifeless
languishing
inside us
with no place to go

until we try again
the next time.

Some Day

A strange time this
made up of opposites with nothing in between
too much time and too much fear of time running out
too many warnings and too little trusting
too much longing and not enough holding
too many memories and not enough now

time has become elastic
it can be pulled this way and that
there is a seemingly inexhaustible supply of it
while the egg timer ticks and ticks
marking time forever lost

electronic watchmen blast blindly
blaring warnings
do this and not that, lest you perish
and in the process, bring others with you
you did not choose to perish in the first place
leave alone ask for company
electronic watchmen
shredding the silence

arms stretch out toward you, yours rise to meet them
nothing moves
except for the furtive inventory
is the other wearing a mask, coming too close
the treasured other now a bearer of ruin
maybe

the worst of it is that you cannot know
what is truth
though unless you know
you cannot be safe
the ease that comes when all that is known
maybe no longer is

still
the sun rises as does the moon
the land is greening and browning
creatures chirp and mate
children giggle

we steal furtive glances at the other's eyes
searching for echo
searching for hope
and so it will come

some day.

Thanks Taking

Have you noticed
how richly we celebrate the special day
we have dedicated to giving thanks?

we spend contemplative moments revisiting
the good things of the past year
also
we treasure the bad things
for not happening

and we feel good about our gratitude

we pride ourselves in the too muchness of food and fun
measuring both by the quantity of leftovers,
and that we kept Uncle George from making a ruckus this year
though the celebrated turkey was not asked
if it would choose to give up its life
for our celebration

so what about this:
what if we held near
the Giving as we do the Thanks
take opportunities for sharing, for soothing
for healing the wounds of others
by our care,
then taking becomes giving
and we will leave the world a kinder place

it is a win-win

Gratitude

Time

I am not going anywhere
in fact, I am very still,
hoping not to be noticed

it is time that makes all the fuss

clearly time has a plan, I just don't know what it is

time gives itself substance by chopping itself into days and nights
    and hours
with stuff in them
but they are just costumes hiding time
ok, I get that

I need to make time visible so that I can remain hidden
so I make rituals for slicing and dicing time's days and nights and
    hours
into palpable functions

eating and not, working to finish something,
to start another thing to finish, and so forth,
then resting
and after that
more eating

some sort of order, seemingly

these chunks of time come at me one by one, big or chopped up,
dressed in different temperatures and feelings

sometimes a day has a wrinkle, a child's birthday, a child's affliction
I want more of one kind of a day, less of another

it doesn't matter to time on the move

so you see,
I am very still

while time's bits and pieces rush past me,
sometimes empty, sometimes pelting me with what can be debris or
    gifts
depending on my orientation or interpretation

more and more chunks of time pile up on the other side of me,
used up
then rearrange themselves behind me into time again

more coming, probably.

Tiny Murders

There is this way of seeing the Other
through the lens of our own design

so the Other becomes a thing of our own making

then we find friends
people who think like we do
people who see the world our way
sharing lenses makes for sharing judgments
of who the Other is
or who we think they should be
and is not

that is when our shared lens makes us feel strong and validated
turns into the ever so barely covered sidelong glances,
the untoward eyeroll, the raised brow, the rueful smile
this secret pleasure of conspirational judgement
the empowering agreement about the flawed Other

treasured
between us and our lens mate

all the while the Other is robbed of their selfhood
is limp and flattened out
devalued of their acts and experiences and meanings
emptied of their humanness
turned into a pile of interchangeable parts
with all those Others of their kind

when we are done the Other is a lifeless thing
shrunken grotesquely under our disapproval
unseen and unknown

these are the endless tiny murders in which we collude

undetectable
unpunished

still everyone dies
a little

and the next time
and the time after that…

and then there is only
nothing

but we can choose

let us put our lens to work
where it will help us see what is true
then our world will become even more beautiful

making ever more life
visible and known and loved.

Toolkit

How we love to touch the stuff in the tool kit our father left us
how reverently we select the just right one
and the job that is waiting to be done
memories of his teachings floating between us

would he be pleased with us
with whom we became?
and why does it matter a lifetime later?
why?

our own tool kit
its contents scattered through our spaces
much of it asking to be gone
because the old us no longer exists
the hairbrush with the horsehair bristles
to tame our then thick unruly hair
these now thinning whisps needing nothing more
than a damp hand running through it

the toothbrush replaced by fizzing cleanser
into which we drop the bank of perfect teeth
not home grown

the harvest of creams and lotions
meant to transform skin chiseled by time
into the smoothly glowing cover
of what it used to be
this army of cosmetics

whispering delusions
into gullible ears

the closet stuffed with what once fit
our bodies or the fashions of the times
now both gone

and then there are the boxes
of love letters
thick with desires and promises
smelling stale

we smile indulgently
maybe give a gentle hug of acceptance
to all that stuff
and possibly even discard
what no longer matters

but do not measure this
against the precious contents
of our father's toolkit
because inside it lives
what made us
who we became
who we are
and so it is.

Trusting

Somehow
the cat, before he became my cat
managed to trust life well enough
that he was willing to give it second chances
hoping for better times

he had neither reason nor experience
for maintaining this belief system
obviously abandoned
he was found trotting along the road
oblivious to danger
while managing to stay safe

he had the use of just one eye
the other shut by a draining infection
malnourished
competing for the limited resources the street offered
eluding its ever present dangers

a bleak way of living
day after day

still, miracles abound, hide in the dark
and sometimes in the heart of humans

and so it was
that Benji came to me
to teach me the lesson
of not giving up trusting

that lesson I needed to learn.

Viewing Point

Have you noticed
how what we call truth
can change, as if by magic
into its opposite?

A huddle of teenagers
invades the crowded Metro
surround me with their foreign language chatter

I am drawn in
try to understand, practice my skills

At the next stop they jump off
I follow eager to hear more

Until I see my emptied wallet lying on the platform
the teens out of sight
swallowed up by the staircase
on their way to boarding the next train

Noting their audacity and my stupidity
My heart breaks just a little
It is not supposed to be that way

But then
I gave you my trust
to trample on and to make me feel small

There are things they need to learn
and so do I

The world had endless space
for
Better.

War and Peace

Unlike the rest we pledged we wouldn't war
We'd hear the other, honor all their needs
would live with understanding, open heart
would blend into a union blessed with peace

and so we did after the knot was tied
at least until we found ourselves alone
had washed the pasted smiles off our stiff faces
and comprehended what we had just done

"you could have been a bit more kind to Rose
you know she was my girlfriend long ago"
"you looked so awkward in your monkey suit
when will you look like who you should be?"

oh well, let's not fight, we're a pair of doves
committed to a life of gentle peace
let's heave our weapons out the door for good
and be kind to each other as we pledged

so we agreed and honored this high goal
at least until the taxi door slammed
and we discovered he had left his wallet
and that her diaphragm was in the nightstand drawer

then we each started an uneasy search
of our own innards, had we erred or worse
should we have run instead of getting tied
to someone so inadequate and plain dumb?

We're at the other end of life now, limping on,
on rage the battles, fights, the struggles, all that stuff
that war is made of and will always be
until the weariest will raise the flag

that white flag of surrender, worn out, done
will simply choose to let it all go down
a truce, an armistice or only a cease-fire
who minds the terms when calm and quiet reign

only of course to once again implode
and set us on the path to war and peace
and oh that energy we waste and generate
how it reminds us that we are alive

Now you might think I have described a lifetime
oh no, this the tale of just one day
and we're quite fine with that because there's love
that one ingredient that runs through all our stuff

So to a multitude of days more like these ones
these so sweetly familiar awful times
without them we'd be lost in empty space
with them we savor all the wealth of life

but please may there be more of one kind, less of the other.

Why

I would like to know what is
On the other side of things like
The wind and forgiveness and death and laughter and time

I would like to know what
draws me to come running to the sweet scent of
a baby's sweaty hair

I would like to know for sure which
crackerjack box has the
just right-for-me prize in it

I would like to know where
goings are coming from and where
all the comings are going

I would like to know how
to be absent from my presence and
to be present at my absence

I would like to know the when
of beginning and of ending
even when they trade places

But most of all I want to know
what is on the other side of
Why.

About the Author

Dr. Heilizer is a clinical psychologist in private practice in Madison, Wisconsin.

www.ingramcontent.com/pod-product-compliance
Lightning Source LLC
Chambersburg PA
CBHW032011080426
42735CB00007B/576